C·L·A·S·S·I·C
Mercedes

CLB 2695
© Colour Library Books Ltd., Godalming, Surrey, England.
This 1991 edition published by Crescent Books,
distributed by Outlet Book Company, Inc., a Random House Company,
225 Park Avenue South, New York, New York 10003.
Printed and bound in Italy
ISBN 0 517 06581 9
8 7 6 5 4 3 2 1

C·L·A·S·S·I·C
Mercedes

CRESCENT BOOKS
NEW YORK

FOREWORD

Anyone who has been to Stuttgart has missed a great opportunity if he has not visited the fascinating Daimler-Benz Museum. Situated inside the factory gates, it contains examples of almost every one of the cars built by Gottlieb Daimler, Karl Benz, or the companies that followed.

Needless to say, for me there has always been particular fascination in the section devoted to the wonderful Mercedes Racing Cars. I wish very much indeed that I had been born a couple of decades earlier and had been given the privilege of racing one of these trend-setting designs. Those who did, tended to win lots of races...

Instead, I shall have to be content with memories of my father Stan Jones, who once raced a frightening aero-engined device called the Maybach Special in honour of its rumbling power-plant.

Maybach, of course, is just one of the names on the illustrious roll of honour in the museum. As you wander around, you will appreciate that Daimler-Benz is more than just a maker of fine road cars: trucks, marine engines, even record-breaking diesels, are all part of the story.

Like Daimler and Benz, my own motoring career was not an immediate "hit". I had to struggle a bit in the beginning, which made success all the more enjoyable. One of the first things I did to celebrate was to order a Mercedes of my own, and when eventually I retired to my farm and other business interests here in Australia, almost the first of my possessions that I had delivered to me was the Mercedes 500 that I had been driving in Europe.

I shan't be staying away from motor sport altogether during my retirement, and I have promised myself at least one trip to Europe every year to renew old friendships and to visit familiar places.

One of those places is Stuttgart, its hard-working Swabian people and the ever fascinating Daimler-Benz Museum. I hope to see much more of them in the years to come.

ALAN JONES
Melbourne, Victoria, 17th January 1982

The illustrations on the facing page show the development in design of the Mercedes radiator shell. From left to right: 1914, 1973, 1926, 1946, 1954, 1961 and 1963. The plain three-pointed star was first used by Daimler on the radiator in 1909, the surrounding ring and name being added in 1916. The top-mounted ringed star appeared in 1921, whilst the laurel leaf and Mercedes-Benz name followed the merger of the two companies in 1926.

1. THE FIRST CARS

The first design for a self-propelled vehicle goes back to 1335, but there is no doubt that Karl Benz and Gottlieb Daimler were the first people to produce a practical horseless carriage. The 1335 design would have been wind-driven, and Leonardo da Vinci also produced a design in the 1400s, but neither of these was ever built. Later came experiments with gunpowder and steam, and even a machine which walked on mechanical legs, but none of them seem to have got very far.

Curiously enough the steam coaches which ran in England from about 1833 were gone by 1867, before the first horseless carriage driven by an internal combustion engine appeared. Karl Benz even gave his name in an indirect way to the fuel—petrol—which powered the new type of vehicle. The word *petrol* came from the Latin words Petra (rock) and *oleum* (oil), and is short for petroleum spirit. A similar fuel, Benzine, was in fact not named after Karl Benz but a professor of the same name at Berlin University, and the compound was known for 50 years before it was used as fuel in this way.

Karl Benz, one of the fathers of the motor-car (curiously, he and Daimler never met) was born in 1844, descended from generations of blacksmiths. His father worked on the railway and died as a result of an accident at work, when he helped lift a locomotive back on the line and caught pneumonia in his open cab afterwards.

Karl went to school in Karlsruhe and started off in the engineering works in that town, building locomotives. Gottlieb Daimler, who was ten years younger than Benz, became chief engineer in the same works three years after Karl had left. This was the nearest they came to meeting.

Benz set up his own business in 1872 in Mannheim, and interested himself in engines from 1877, the year when Nikolaus Otto patented his design for the four-stroke engine, forcing everyone else to use two-strokes.

(1) The Benz Velo Comfortable of 1894/5 had a rear-mounted single cylinder engine producing 1.5 horsepower and capable of 30 km/h. (2) The 1892 Daimler, pictured in the Black Forest region, featured primitive bicycle-type forks to the front wheels operated by a tiller mechanism. (3) A steering wheel was used on the early Benz of 1891, which had a single-cylinder rear engine and vis-à-vis seating. (4) Gottlieb Daimler and Wilhelm Maybach (at the controls), demonstrate an 1981 Daimler fitted with lamps and a hood.

(5) Daimler's very first vehicle was the wooden-framed motorcycle of 1885. The 0.5 horsepower single-cylinder engine could reach 12 km/h at 600 rpm. (6) The first Benz car of 1886 had a rear-mounted single-cylinder 1 litre engine with chain drive, which produced 0.89 horsepower at 400 rpm to give a top speed of 15 km/h. (7) Daimler's famous 'steel-wheeler' of 1889 still used bicycle forks, but now a twin-cylinder 0.97 litre rear engine gave an output of 1.65 horsepower at 920 rpm, and a speed of 18 km/h. (8) The Benz Victoria of 1893 was a motoring milestone, its 2.92 litre single-cylinder engine producing a top speed of 25 km/h. (9) A purpose built vehicle rather than a horseless carriage, this 1886 Benz three-wheeler used electric ignition instead of the crude hot-tube. (10) Although there had been earlier machines, this Benz 'Patent-Motorwagen' of 1886 was claimed to be the world's first practical automobile.

5

7

8

10

THE FIRST CARS

Benz' first engine ran on New Year's Eve, 1879. By 1884 he realised that a lawsuit against Otto's four-stroke patent would succeed, and transferred his efforts to a four-stroke engine which would be the heart of an automobile, unlike Daimler and Maybach who did not think of an entire automobile as a concept until 1889.

Benz' first engine produced 0.8 horse power at 250 revolutions a minute, and was water-cooled. It featured trembler-coil ignition from a battery. His 1886 'patent motor-car' was a tricycle with the engine at the rear, and a horizontal flywheel which could be spun for starting. The engine drove a belt to a shaft which had chains to the bicycle wheels through a differential. Benz was ahead of Daimler with his electric ignition, while Daimler used the crude hot-tube sticking out of the cylinder, upon which a blowlamp was played.

Benz also made his own sparking-plugs until Bosch took over the production. His first drives in the Ringstrasse on July 3, 1886, passed almost unnoticed except by the local newspaper. Passing pedestrians apparently thought it all very funny, as Benz had problems, hard to solve away from his workshop and without tools. But by 1888 he was showing an improved model at the Munich Engine Show, on sale for 2,000 marks, running costs put at 30 pfennigs an hour.

Newspapers were already calling it a 'petrol engine' rather than a 'gas engine' as it originally was. His car was said to do 16 kilometres an hour, but there were no buyers and the German Yearbook for Natural Science for 1888 said: 'Benz has also made a petrol car which caused some storm at the Munich Exposition. This employment of the petrol engine will probably be no more promising for the future than the use of the steam engine for road travel.'

In August 1888 Benz' wife with her two sons Eugen and Richard sneaked off at 5 a.m. while father was asleep, to drive in the new car from Mannheim to Pforzheim. The leather brake shoe wore out and a cobbler fitted a new one in Bauschlott, Frau Benz solving a short-circuit problem with her garter elastic. They repaired the chains and unblocked the fuel line, and arrived feeling very pleased with themselves, but a telegram to father Benz brought the reply: 'Return driving chains at once. They are needed for Munich exhibition car.' The chains went back by train, but he sent new ones for the return journey.

But Benz' partners in the Mannheim company, the Rheinische Gasmotorenfabrik, Max Kaspar Rose and Fredrich Wilhelm Esslinger told him: 'Herr Benz, we've now made a nice pile of money, but you had better keep your fingers out of that motorcar or you'll lose everything.'

On May 1, 1890 his partners left and he found two new ones. By 1891 he had produced his first four-wheel car, the Benz Viktoria, which

1

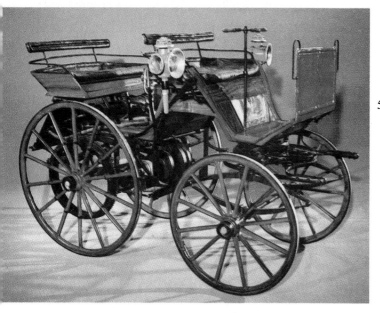

has become a motoring landmark. With this model he abandoned the horizontal flywheel—he had been afraid of gyroscopic action with it vertical—and used a three horse-power engine. It used the forerunner of the modern jet carburettor and had variable gear ratios, by movable belt.

In July 1894 an Austrian, Theodor von Liebieg, made the first long drive in a Viktoria from Reichenberg, Bohemia via Mannheim and Gondorf to Rheims in France and back. The motocar was on its way. From the Viktoria sprung the Velo, which could do 20 kilometres an hour, and had three speeds and reverse. It was the first 'mass-produced' car, and in 1895 out of Benz' production of 135 cars 62 were Velos.

By 1899 Benz had made 2,000 cars and was the world's biggest auto maker. He was also entering cars in competitions like the 54-kilometre Berlin-Potsdam-Berlin race in which three Benz cars ran. The firm was reorganised once again, in 1899, and Max Kaspar Rose, who had shown so little faith in the automobile, came back as an investor and director.

2. DAIMLER THE PIONEER

Gottlieb Daimler was born on March 17, 1834 in Schorndorf in the Rems valley, once called Wurttemberg's 'Little Garden of Paradise'. The family name was originally Teimbler or Teumler, then Daumler and

ultimately Daimler. His father ran a baker's shop and wine bar combined, and Gottlieb started his working life apprenticed to a gunsmith. He also attended the School for Advanced Training in the Industrial Arts at Stuttgart, taking lessons in the evenings and on Sundays.

His first job was in a factory near Strasbourg, making railway carriages, goods vans, tenders and various other kinds of machinery. The day began at 5 a.m. and sometimes ran on into the night, and there was not much time for sleep. Gottlieb was also still taking technical instruction and learning French. He became foreman at 22 when the factory began building locomotives.

Daimler then won leave of absence for two years' study at the Stuttgart Polytechnic to learn physics, chemistry, engine design, engineering, economics and English. He left in 1859 at 25 years of age, and went back briefly to Grafenstaden, but had lost interest in steam engines and felt that what was needed was an engine which would start instantly without the need for preparation, and he left for new fields, visiting Paris and London.

He worked in Leeds and Manchester on textile and shipbuilding

(1) The horizontally opposed twin-cylinder 'boxer' engine of the Benz 'Mylord' Coupé of 1896-99 gave the car a top speed of 40 km/h. (2) This 1903 Mercedes (the name was adopted in 1901) was known as the Kettenwagen Coupé, and featured a four-cylinder engine. (3) The four-cylinder 40 horsepower

Mercedes Simplex of 1902 had many novel features and was capable of 70 km/h. (4) Daimler's first car, a converted horse-carriage with a single-cylinder rear engine, first ran in 1886. (5) A 4.5 litre four-cylinder front-mounted engine powered the Benz Phaeton Landaulette of 1909.

(1) The Mercedes Reisewagen of 1903 used a four-cylinder 9.23 litre engine as in the Simplex, and could reach 80 km/h. (2) This short wheel-base Benz Spider of 1902, although sporting in look, was powered by a small 15 horsepower engine. (3) The Mercedes Simplex, made between 1902-4, was not exclusively a sporting car as this bus-like limousine on the 60 horsepower chassis demonstrates. This vehicle was powered by a 5.3 litre version of the four-cylinder engine.

1

2

3

machinery and locomotives, then returned to Germany to a designing job on tools, mills and turbines. He moved to manage another engineering works, and was married in 1867 to Emma Kurz, and then met Wilhelm Maybach who was to become a name in automotive history.

In 1869 Daimler became director of a Karlsruhe engineering plant and hired Maybach to work for him, before moving to a company making Otto gas engines in 1872, taking Maybach with him. But there was a problem with the gas engines, which needed a ceiling up to 13 feet high, too much for small workshops, so Daimler was given a brief to develop a petrol engine.

Otto produced a drawing for his four-stroke engine in May, 1876, and Daimler ordered some electrical ignition systems, but dropped them in favour of the crude hot-tube. But there were personal clashes between Daimler, Otto, and Eugen Langen, so Gottlieb was sent out of the way on a tour of Russia, leaving the company on his return to Germany.

From a factory employing 300 men making 600 engines a year Daimler moved his activities to the garden shed of his new home in Canstatt, but he was now 48 years of age and needed relief from tension. Maybach came to join him, and they set about the design and production of a vehicle engine, which they achieved by 1883.

(4) A splendid 1908 Mercedes Edwardian tourer with gleaming brass fittings and a dog mascot on the radiator. Note the lack of door on the driver's side; a common omission on contemporary cars.

(5) This vast 1910 limousine had right-hand drive and enclosed passenger accommodation, although the chauffeur's compartment remained open.

The air-cooled design gave place to water-cooling, although the air-cooled version was fitted to a wooden-framed motor-cycle, Daimler's first vehicle, in 1885.

Gottlieb then ordered a normal horse-drawn coach from Wimpff & Son and to maintain secrecy said it was a present for his wife. The engine, together with the radiator, was fitted in the rear. Maybach drove the first Daimler car in the works and the garden outside, but Gottlieb's thoughts were on putting the engine on rails or in the water; perhaps even in the air.

The first engine was a single-cylinder, but by 1889 Daimler had a V-twin, which sold widely in France. He also made a flight in 1888 in a balloon driven by one of his engines, and sold many for use in boats. The V-twin gave twice the power for the same weight, an important

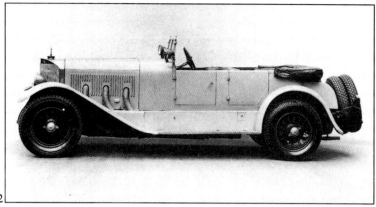

lesson in automotive engineering. The four-speed 'Steel wheeler' car of 1889 was shown at the Paris World Fair, and was clearly no longer a horseless carriage but a purpose-made motor-car capable of 18 km/hr from its 1.65 horsepower twin cylinder engine.

At the Paris fair a journalist commented that Daimler was 'germinating the seed of the modern technological revolution'. The French firm of Panhard and Levassor began making their own cars with Daimler's engines, which was the foundation of his fortune. In the United States the great piano maker, William Steinway, was Daimler's selling agent. In November 1890 Daimler founded Daimler-Motoren-Gesellschaft with two partners.

Two of the Daimler-powered Panhard cars won joint first prize in the world's first motor race, a run organised by a Paris newspaper from Paris to Rouen, a distance of 78.5 miles, at a speed of 12.5 mph, which was slower than the cyclists. This was in 1894, and the following year Panhard and Peugeot, both using Daimler engines, won top prizes in the 745-mile Paris-Bordeaux-Paris event. Panhard also won the 1,080-mile Paris-Marseilles-Paris race.

An Englishman born in Hamburg, Frederick Richard Simms, took out a licence to exploit Daimler patents in the British Empire. This was the start of the Daimler Motor Company Ltd, which eventually became quite distinct from the German Daimler-Benz firm. They made cars in Coventry. Meanwhile in Germany power outputs were going up, and Daimler abandoned the belt-drive transmission which he had tried and went back to gears.

From 1898 engines began to have four cylinders, and the following year Daimler adopted electric ignition, convinced of its virtues over the hot-tube. But Gottlieb's health was failing, although he lived to see

The first in a famous line of Mercedes supercharged touring cars. (1) The 1928 7.1 litre 225 horsepower model with six-cylinder engine. (2) This powerful tourer, known as the 28/95 was an early version of the 7 litre sports car, as can be seen from the radiator design. (3)

The legendary Grosser Mercedes Super Straight Eight Pullman Limousine was made from 1903-1938 and had a top speed of 160 km/h. (4) The Grosser Mercedes in 7/8 seater cabriolet form was much favoured by latter-day VIPs.

his son Paul put in charge of the Austrian Daimler factory. He died on March 6, 1900, just one year before the Mercedes car, to which he had made such a contribution, came into being.

His son Paul did not take over the Austrian plant until 1902, as he was busy with the Mercedes development; his brother Adolf took over until he was ready, but died early in 1913.

3. MERCEDES FINDS ITS NAME

Maybach and Otto have already come into the story of Daimler and Benz, and Maybach was associated with Gottlieb up until the time of the latter's death, mostly as his chief designer. Otto was not as closely involved after making his big contribution in the invention of the four-stroke cycle, which is now universally used in the internal combustion engine, apart from those in some motor-cycles. Pollution laws have effectively outlawed the two-stroke from cars.

Maybach had long been the designing genius and took over when Daimler died. One of his briefs was to build a faster car than those being made by Panhard and Levassor, a project in which he was egged on by Emil Jellinek, the Austrian consul general in Nice and also a successful entrepreneur.

(5) The 1930 Grosser Mercedes in Kaiserwagen form, with Walter Lange at the wheel. (6) The conventionally styled Benz Phaeton was powered by a four-cylinder 10/18 horsepower engine and was made between 1908 and 1912. (7) The three-axle Type 500 G4 W31 made from 1933-1939 was designed for cross-country work, the 5 litre 100 horsepower engine giving a top speed of 65 km/h. (8) Built expressly for military use, this 170 V special light four-seater used a 1.7 litre 38 horsepower four-cylinder unit. (9) The highly successful straight-eight engine was used in the 1928 Nurnburg 18/80, here shown in Pullman Limousine form.

The 1898 Daimler 23 horsepower racer had beaten the opposition in races on March 21 and 24, but Panhard were ahead again in the Paris-Bordeaux and the Tour de France, using the Daimler Phoenix engine introduced in 1893, with a two-cyliner in-line layout and the Maybach spray carburetter which adjusted the supply of mixture according to the engine's needs.

In the 1900 Speed Week at Nice a Daimler works driver, Wilhelm Bauer, had a fatal accident in the 23 horsepower model on the La Turbie hill-climb course on March 30. Jellinek, who was the Daimler agent and sold cars to all his wealthy titled friends, demanded a safer car with a lower centre of gravity and longer wheelbase, but also with more power.

Jellinek had already been driving in races under the pseudonym 'Mercedes', the name of one of his pretty daughters. In the 1901 Nice meeting he appeared with the first Mercedes car, successor to the Phoenix and sometimes known as the 35 horsepower. It was the foundation of the modern motor-car, with a pressed steel frame, honeycomb radiator, steering wheel instead of tiller, four-speed gearbox with gate-change, mechanically-operated valves and magneto ignition. It also had both transmission and wheel brakes.

Mechanically-operated valves which we now take for granted were something of a novelty, as most valves on early cars were 'automatic', that is operated, in the case of the inlet, by the suction of the piston against a light spring. The speed of the engine was controlled not by a throttle as today, but by varying the lift of the inlet valves, which called for considerable driving skill. But the new Mercedes was fast and a tremendous advance on previous models.

MERCEDES FINDS ITS NAME

Showing its race breeding this 1921 Benz sportscar, known as the 6/18, used a four-cylinder engine that gave a top speed of 90 km/h. Its features included magneto ignition and Zenith carburettor, and it was also available as a tourer. (2) The 1914 French Grand Prix was a major success for Mercedes, where their four-cylinder 4.5 litre cars finished 1-2-3 in front of a fiercely partisan French crowd. The engine had four valves and three plugs per cylinder, and a single overhead camshaft, developing 115 horsepower at 3200 rpm. Unlike the other competitors, brakes were fitted only to the rear wheels of the Daimler powered cars.

Jellinek ordered 36 of the new cars in return for an exclusive agency for Austria-Hungary, France, Belgium and America. In those countries it would be called Mercedes after his 11-year-old daughter, and in other countries 'the New Daimler'. In the Nice races from March 25 to 29 the new car beat all others. It also had good road-holding, comfort, good handling, and solid construction. It was a sensation. The following year the name Mercedes was registered as a trademark and became the *marque* name for Daimlers, although the company is still to this day officially called Daimler-Benz.

Maybach was now a name to be conjured with. The company's payroll had increased in numbers since Daimler's death from 340 to 2,200 by 1903. Camille Jenatzy won the Gordon-Bennett cup offered by the American newpaper owner, driving a sixty horsepower Mercedes. During preparations for this race a fire destroyed the Canstatt factory

(3) With supercharger engaged, the 24/100/140 *sportscar produced* 145 *horsepower at 3000 rpm from its* 6.2 *litre six-cylinder engine, the top speed being 125 km/h. (4) Front view of the all-conquering 1914 Grand Prix car.*

whose brother Adolf became chief engineer at Unterturkheim.

Wilhelm Maybach had also designed airship engines for Count Zeppelin, who built a factory on Lake Constance at Friedrichshafen, which was run by Karl Maybach, his son. Maybach died in 1929, having collaborated with Gottlieb Daimler from 1865 to 1900.

Nikolaus Otto had also played a role in the development of the crude early cars up to the Mercedes standard which gave direction to the rest of the industry. In 1877 he had asked Eugen Langen, another pioneer who had helped Daimler on his way, to get the opinion of Werner Siemens—the electrical specialist—on electric ignition. Siemens gave a demonstration and Daimler placed an order, but tests were unsatisfactory.

Eugen Langen's brother Gustav, tried to overcome the clash between Otto and Daimler which made 'a fruitful atmosphere of working together between colleagues impossible' at the Gasmotoren-Fabrik Deutz, in 1880. It was Gustav who suggested Daimler be put in charge of a foreign subsidiary company, and led to his trip to Moscow by way of Berlin and Vienna. At the same time they suggested opening a factory in St. Petersburg (now Leningrad) with Daimler in charge, but meanwhile his contract was cancelled.

The personality clashes between the great pioneers of the motor-car eventually led to moves which set Daimler up on his own with Maybach and proved to be to the good of the future development of the new industry.

so the planned move to Unterturkheim (where Daimler-Benz still are) had to be advanced.

Maybach developed the Ninety and then the six-cylinder Seventy, but Max Duttenhofer, the chairman, died and Maybach was not on good terms with his successor Wilhelm Lorenz, who had earlier refused Daimler's request to put Maybach in charge of engineering. So on April 1, 1907, Maybach left the company. He was succeeded by Paul Daimler,

(1) Dating from 1922, this 6/25 Mercedes limousine used a four-cylinder 1.5 litre engine. (2) Steering-column gear change was a feature of the 1952 170 DS four-cylinder diesel model. (3) The elegant drophead coupé body on the 1958 220S six-cylinder Mercedes. (4) The Grosser Mercedes 770K Pullman Limousine was a 7.7 litre eight-cylinder giant introduced in 1938.

(5) The Mercedes 200 diesel from 1965-68 was particularly successful as a taxi. (6) With engine revealed, the supercharger on the 1927 7.1 litre SSK can clearly be seen. (7) Introduced in 1956, the four-cylinder 190 model was the workhorse of the late fifties. (8) The 1951/2 300S convertible heralded the return of the company to the 'quality' car market.

4. THE THREE-POINTED STAR

By 1902 the great names had been dropped from the radiator badges of the cars and the new *marque* Mercedes was in being, but it was not until 1909 that the famous three-pointed star badge appeared. Mercedes is really a Spanish name meaning 'Mercy'. Daimler in Canstatt and Benz in Mannheim has been working only 60 miles apart, but still did not meet.

The original Mannheim cars bore a circular badge with gear-teeth around the perimeter, with the words 'Original Benz' one under the other. This was around 1903, and then in 1909 a laurel wreath was added around the rim and the gear teeth dropped, along with the word 'Original'. Daimler cars were already using the Mercedes name from 1902, set inside an oval badge.

6

7

8

Daimler was already dead but his sons Paul and Adolf, when looking for a badge design, or logo as we would now call it, recalled that their father had once sent back home a postcard to his wife with a guiding star drawn over their house in Deutz, with an indication that this star would one day mark the ascendancy of his work.

The directors of Daimler-Gesellschaft welcomed the idea and in June 1909 they registered both a three-pointed and a four-pointed star as trademarks. Although both forms were patented, only the three-pointed star was used in the form of an embossed radiator badge. The three points of the star were intended to represent transport motorisation on land, sea and in the air.

The star appeared in various forms over the years, and in 1916 was placed inside a circle with a border containing four stars at the top with the word Mercedes balancing them at the bottom, or alternatively the name of the Daimler factory at either Unterturkheim or Berlin-Marienfelde was added as well. Then in 1921 it was announced that the three-pointed star would be adopted as a radiator emblem, and two years later it was registered.

Up to 1924 the two firms, Daimler and Benz, were in competition, but in that year they joined in a working agreement to coordinate design, production, buying and selling, as well as publicity, but they kept different trademarks.

Two years later, in 1926, the two companies amalgamated to form Daimler-Benz A.G. and the new trademark was the three-pointed star inside a circle with a border enclosing the two names Mercedes and Benz with branches of laurel joining the words at either end. This has been kept, and the three-pointed star is now said to stand for service and the name for pioneering spirit and tradition.

The first models after that were the Mannheim and Stuttgart. The latter was also called the Type 200, a six-cylinder upright saloon of 1.98 litres producing 38 bhp at 3,500 rpm and a top speed of 80 km/h, and it had a spare wheel mounted on the rear of the vehicle. The Mannheim name carried on for several years on different models, in 1930 on the sporting 370S drophead coupé. In deference to modern safety regulations the three-pointed star on the radiator now bends over if pushed.

The following year saw the advent of the famous sporting line which culminated in the 38/250, starting with the 26/180 Model S with a supercharger on a six-cylinder engine of 6.79 litres offering 180 bhp at 3,000 rpm and 100 miles an hour, a fabulous speed for its day. There was a bewildering multiplicity of models in those years, from the Super

THE THREE-POINTED STAR

1

2

3

(1) The supercharged 6.8 litre 26/120/180S sportscar of 1927 was capable of 160 km/h. (2) Although somewhat more impressive, this 1937 320 model, with its six-cylinder 3.2 litre engine, was slower than its sporting predecessor. (3) The sober appearance of this 1934 550K saloon belied the 165 km/h top speed it was capable of. (4) The 170 V, here in limousine form, was a successful and long-lived, if unexciting car. Introduced in 1935 it appeared in a variety of different guises. (5) The 170S cabriolet version was added to the Mercedes range in 1949. Engine capacity was now 1.8 litres, and at 4000 rpm the top speed was 120 km/h. It was this model, more than any other, that

re-established the reputation of Mercedes as a top-class car manufacturer after the war. (6) The 1928 Nurnburg 460 model had an in-line eight-cylinder engine, and a somewhat sedate top speed of 100 km/h at 3400 rpm.

Mercedes eight-cylinder of 1930 with 7.66 litre engine and supercharger in a vast saloon body, down to the little 130H of 1933 which was a 1.3 litre four, with a modest 26 horsepower and 92 km/h top speed.

In the 'thirties the company was making cars with four, six and eight cylinders and had standardised on the performance and luxury image which later became its hallmark, perhaps because it had to merge two conflicting product lines and two boards of management and ways of thinking. Although the open touring cars had been superseded by

and fulfilled the same role. Although outside Germany Mercedes have always been seen as purveyors of sporting and luxury cars, in their home country they also supply the taxis and more humble transport for the masses. A two-seater version of the 1933 130H was also produced powered by an overhead camshaft engine producing 55 bhp.

In contrast to this essentially simple, practical vehicle for country dwellers, Mercedes also marketed a front-engined car, the 170V (*Vor* for front-engined) which was even more successful than the 130H, and

5

5

saloons, there have always been drophead coupés in the range and two-door sporting cars as well as the businessman's express.

The little 130H (H for *Hintern* or rear-engine) came from Czechoslovakia, was designed by Carl Ledwinka of Tatra, and had a large tube running down the centre as a backbone and independent suspension. The engine was a simple side-valve and the whole concept was wide of the Mercedes image, but it was simple, gave a good ride on rough country roads, and had an overdrive fourth gear which could be engaged without using the clutch.

The 130H was in many ways a predecessor of the Volkswagen

there was also a 170H with the bigger engine. These model numbers were supposed to represent the engine size in cubic centimetres divided by ten, but in modern times Mercedes type-numbers have become very confusing as the same ones are used over again for different models.

There was also a convertible version of the 170V in 1935 with the same four-cylinder 1.7 litre engine producing 38 horsepower at 3,200 rpm and giving a top speed of 110 km/h. This was a pretty car with outside pram-irons and a forerunner of the later 190 and subsequent models.

THE SPORTING SIDE

(1) A historic picture of Prince Heinrich of Prussia driving a Benz in the Herkomer trials of 1906. (2) Caracciola at the wheel of his powerful W25 car seen heading the field in the Italian Grand Prix at Monza in 1934. (3) The victorious Mercedes team pose for photographs at the Untertürkheim factory following their famous 1-2-3 win in the French Grand Prix of 1914. (4) Otto Merz, pictured with Ernst Hemminger in car No. 15, won the 1925 Solitude race in his four-cylinder 2 litre supercharged Mercedes. Karl Sailer and his brother Richard are shown in the No. 14 car.

5. THE SPORTING SIDE

Mercedes had been involved in motor-sport right from the Benz and Daimler days of the 1894 Paris-Rouen race, and the first Mercedes under that new name was conceived as a sporting machine. It is no surprise therefore that the company has been very successful in every form of competition, from rallying to Grand Prix racing. The company worked to the formula: 'The racing car of today is the touring car of tomorrow'.

Mercedes took many records before 1939, the first with the then-new Mercedes 35 horsepower in 1901 at Nice, with a one-mile speed of 79.7 km/h. The following year this went up to 83.2 km/h.

After many more records the highest speed ever on a highway up to that time was established by Rudi Caracciola in 1939 on the autobahn at 432.4 km/h, to take Class B (5 to 8 litres) records for the flying mile and flying kilometre.

In the stage between the wars, victories were seen in the Targa Florio, German Grand Prix, Tourist Trophy, Grand Prix of Ireland, Argentine Grand Prix, Finnish Grand Prix and many sports car races. In these races the SSKL sports car in racing trim, often with the legendary Caracciola at the wheel, was competing against Grand Prix cars. He was known as the Rainmaster, and his victories in the wet in such a big, heavy car have become historic feats.

(5) An atmospheric shot of the speeding entrants in the 1930 Monaco round-the houses Grand Prix. It is interesting to note the predominance of Bugatti cars, distinguishable by their horse-shoe shaped radiator shells. Mercedes cars were nevertheless also present, and Caracciola finished in third place despite several pit stops. (6) Mercedes W25 cars form the front row of the starting grid for the Monaco Grand Prix in 1935. The race was won by Luigi Fagioli in the No. 4 car. Hans Nibel, who had designed the car, died in 1934 without witnessing its considerable success.

THE SPORTING SIDE

(1) Rudolf Caracciola at the wheel of his SSK sportscar in the Italian Mille Miglia race of 1931. Driving single-handed, he won the event in record time, completing the 1635 km course in 16 hrs. 10 minutes at an average speed of 101 km/h. With supercharging, the six-cylinder car developed a reputed 300 horsepower. (2) The fastest race of 1937 was won by Hermann Lang in his specially streamlined W15 Mercedes on the Berlin Avus circuit at a speed of 261.7 km/h. The picture below shows Caracciola in the same race, also at the wheel of a Mercedes-Benz. The following year he was to set the fastest speed ever achieved on a road of 432.7 km/h.

1

2

U 17172

(3) The picture shows Manfred von Brauchitsch during the 1939 Belgrade Grand Prix. (4) Luigi Fagioli pulls into the pits for fuel and a tyre change during the 1934 Italian Grand Prix. (5) The 1928 SSK 7.1 litre sportscar powered by a supercharged straight-six engine, was capable of an incredible 250 km/h. (6) Pictured at the Monza circuit during the 1923 European Grand Prix, run over 800 km, is the unusual tear-drop shaped 2 litre rear-engined Benz car.

In the formula restricting weight to 750 kg, from 1934-7, Mercedes were supreme with the W25, giving 354 bhp from 3.36 litres. In following years it went up to 4.3 litres (462 bhp) and then 4.7 litres (494 bhp) from its supercharged, straight-eight engine. But in 1937 came the W125, which produced a massive 592 bhp from 5.66 litres at 5,800 rpm, in one of the most successful racing cars ever, and certainly the most powerful.

It had four valves per cylinder operated by twin overhead camshafts, and a De Dion rear axle, little used in racing. It was capable of 200 mph and could spin its tyres on dry concrete at 150 mph. Few men

THE SPORTING SIDE

Belgian Grand-Prix, which he won, Moss coming in second. (5) Moss and Fangio pictured after their victory in the 1955 British Grand Prix at Aintree. (6) A happy Caracciola after his 1935 win in the Tripoli Grand Prix. (7) The legendary Neubauer (right) congratulates his team after their 1955 British Grand Prix victory. (8) Fangio, having won the 1955 Dutch Grand Prix, shakes hands with second-placed team-mate Stirling Moss. (9) The experimental C111-1V, driven by Dr. Hans Niebold, established five world records in 1979.

(1) The Streamliner W196 Mercedes made its debut at Rheims in the 1954 French Grand Prix, and is seen here alongside the open-wheeled Maserati of Ascari. Fangio and Kling took the cars to a 1-2 victory. (2) In 1955 Stirling Moss joined the Mercedes team as number two to Fangio. (3) The 1955 Italian Grand Prix, held on the banked Monza track, was won by Fangio, Moss having retired. (4) Fangio at the wheel of his open-wheeled W196 during the 1955

could drive it to its capacity. One of them was Caracciola, and the duels between the Mercedes and the competing German Auto Union, which both eclipsed all others, were an awesome sight.

In its ultimate form in 1937 the W125 with enclosed wheels in a stream-lined shell unlike the open-wheeled W125—both models had the same designation—put out 646 bhp from the same 5.66 litres and was capable of 330 km/h. But there was yet another monster to come, the W154 for the new formula limiting engine size to three litres supercharged. For this, the designers produced an engine of half the old size, giving 480 bhp and 400 km/h, from 1938-40.

Also worth a mention are the two special cars built for the Tripoli Grand Prix, which Mercedes had won in 1935, '37 and '38. Suddenly, to help the existing 1.5 litre Italian cars, the rules called for a 1.5 litre limit,

8

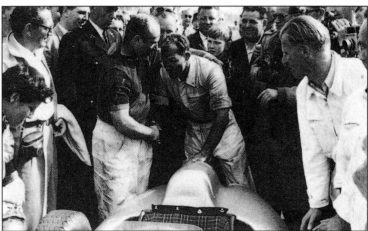

THE SPORTING SIDE

(1) The 3 litre V-12 W154/M racing car of 1939 had a top speed of 320 km/h. **(2)** With financial assistance from the government, the 1934 W25 was designed and built in record time, under the direction of Hans Nibel. The eight-cylinder 3.56 litre dohc engine developed 325 bhp at 5800 rpm. **(3)** The historic 4.5 litre racer that won the 1914 French Grand Prix. **(4)** Stirling Moss in thoughtful mood as mechanics attend to his car. **(5)** The W154/M of 1939 in action. Its twelve-cylinder engine

produced 483 bhp at 7500 rpm. **(6)** Fangio disliked the enclosed wheel design of the 1954 W196 streamliner, as this made judgement more difficult. The car had a five-speed gearbox, and the eight-cylinder engine produced 290 bhp at 8500 rpm. **(7)** As an open wheel car, the 2.5 litre 1954/55 W196 became popular with the drivers and proved successful for Fangio in the 1954 season. It had swing-axle rear and independent front suspension.

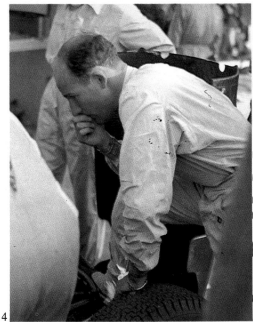

5

6

7

but Mercedes produced two cars in time for the event and finished first and second (Hermann Lang and Rudolf Caracciola), winning speed 197.8 km/h, fastest lap 211.6 km/h. These two cars still exist.

The W154's produced for the 1938 three-litre formula were 12-cylinder machines, overshadowed only by the 1939 version, the W163 with two-stage supercharging, which could do 195 mph at the rate of one mile per gallon. One-quarter of the car's starting weight was made up of fuel. The 1.5 litre cars built for Tripoli looked like the W163, but had two-stage supercharged V8 engines and were known as the W165. From this tiny engine they gave 254 bhp at a phenomenal (for the time) 8,000 rpm.

Mercedes came back after the war with the 300SL sports car, which won Le Mans, The Carrera Panamericana, and the Swiss and German sports car grands prix of 1952. This was the model with gullwing doors, which swung up instead of out, and a spaceframe chassis.

Then came the racing version, the 300SLR with an eight-cylinder engine and a lot more power. The six-cylinder 300SL had three litres and 215 bhp at 5,800 rpm, but the racer had 310 bhp and 260 km/h, peaking at 7,500 rpm. In 1954 the company came back to Grand Prix racing into the 2.5 litre formula, in the year which was the 60th anniversary of the first motor race in which they had done so well.

Their chosen instrument was the W196 with eight cylinders and 290 bhp at 8,700 rpm. It won most of the grands prix and the world championship for Juan Manuel Fangio, who held the title five times. Stirling Moss also drove for Mercedes, and in 1955 won the Mille Miglia at 157.65 km/h with Fangio second.

THE SPORTING SIDE

But 1955 was also the year in which Pierre Levegh crashed at Le Mans in a 300 SLR, killing about 90 people in the crowd, and Mercedes pulled out of racing, although they won the world championship of makes that year for sports racing cars. Up to that time 2,005 different drivers had won 4,400 races or events for Mercedes in 68 years of competition.

They were directed by the imposing figure of Neubauer, who bullied his men to win and was a legend on the racing circuits of the world, imposing team discipline and brooking no arguments. His drivers included Kling, Taruffi, von Trips, Gendebien, Hermann and Collins in addition to those already mentioned.

In earlier days there were the red-bearded Jenatzy, laughing

Lautenschlager, Ralph da Palma, Christian Werner, and Rosemeyer who died in an autobahn record attempt. It has been a brave history of intrepid men and mighty machines.

6. THE DAIMLER-BENZ MUSEUM

The Daimler-Benz museum in the headquarters at Unterturkheim is a visual demonstration of the continuity of the work of the two founders

(1, 2 and overleaf) The ultimate vintage road-going Mercedes was the 1929 six-cylinder 7 litre supercharged 38/250SSK. (3, 4, 5) The Targa Florio 28/95 of 1924 was also a seven litre six-cylinder car but without supercharger. It was the ancestor of the 1929 blown SSK model.

1

2

(1) The convertible, drophead coupé and cabriolet bodies have always been effective on the various Mercedes chassis. This version, on a Mannheim 75 horsepower car of 1931, has fine lines and a solid, heavily-lined German type hood. The six-cylinder 3.7 litre car was known as the 15/75 or 370K (short) or 370S (sports), and was built by an outside coachbuilder. (2) The 540K was the final

statement of the supercharged sporting car. This 1936 model produced 115 horsepower normally aspirated or 180 horsepower with supercharger in use, from its 5.4 litres. Maximum power was at 3600 rpm and a top speed of 170 km/h was claimed. (3) It is interesting to compare this 1936 Sedanca Drophead

500K, the coachwork by Corsica, with the more powerful 540K shown (2). (4, 5) Although somewhat dull by comparison, this 1937 saloon type 320 nevertheless has solid, elegant lines and twin side-mounted spare wheels. The 3.2 litre engine was a straight-six capable of 126 km/h.

chassis on view illustrate the gradual construction change from the frame with rigid axles to the first swing axle and then the frame floor unit with subframe that we know today.

Motor racing is well represented in the museum, from the 1894 Paris-Rouen victory to the 300SLR which swept all before it up to 1955. Landmarks include the 1914 cars which finished 1-2-3 in the French Grand Prix to the disgust of the crowds, the 1911 Blitzen Benz, and what is called the compressor (supercharger) epoch of the SSKL which performed so well in the hands of Rudi Caracciola.

Apart from illustrating the racing history and technical progress, the museum also houses such milestone cars as the C111, first seen at the Frankfurt show in 1969. This two-seater coupé was purely experimental, a workshop on wheels in which the engineers could test their theories and individual pieces of design and equipment.

The mobile laboratory not only provided testing for stress on bodywork and chassis components, but was powered by a unique engine, a four-rotor Wankel rotary piston engine producing 350 brake

over 90 years of motoring, and shows how the car has switched from being a luxury to a fundamental element of commercial and social life. There are replicas of the very first vehicles and genuine early engines, but unfortunately there is no example of the very first Mercedes, the 35 horsepower of 1901, although there is a 1902 version in the 28/32 model.

But the Mannheim and Stuttgart are both represented, and such classic machines as the 540K, a two-seater version of which recently sold in the United States for more than $400,000 to a collector. The various

The 300SL is a rare and historic model that was made both as a conventional convertible and the more exciting hard-top with the distinctive gull-wing doors. The open sports version is the rarer. Developed from the racing version of 1952, these 1954 cars were powered by a six-cylinder 3 litre engine producing 215 bhp at 5800 rpm with a top speed of 260 km/h. The 300SLR racing version had an eight-cylinder engine that produced 310 bhp at 7500 rpm. Whereas the early racers used carburettors, all the road-going cars were fuel-injected.

1

2

3

4

5

horsepower. The advantages of the Wankel were that it had few moving parts, eliminating the crankshaft, connecting rods, valves and normal pistons, but in service it proved to have problems with sealing and with the toxic content of the exhaust, plus heavy fuel consumption and is now in production by only one or two manufacturers in the automobile industry.

The C111 was revolutionary in more senses than just in the engine department, as it had a steel frame floor unit with an aerodynamically-designed resin body reinforced with glassfibre, with the power unit placed in front of the rear axle, so that it was mid-engined and endowed with prodigious handling properties. It taught lessons valuable both in racing and in production cars, far beyond the limits of what can be learned on a test track or at the bench.

Safety is a fairly modern preoccupation, but Daimler-Benz have

been doing research in this field since the 'thirties, which is not generally known. They started with independent frontwheel suspension and made many tests from 1939 up to 1948. The following year (1949) the safety door-lock was developed, and in 1959 the body with crushable zones front and rear and a rigid centre cabin for the passengers was offered.

In 1971 the programme included an Experimental Safety Vehicle (ESV), brought into use for testing new devices and ideas in a continuing stream as they are designed and developed for production use. Mercedes have been at the forefront of safety measures in their cars, limited only by the technical and financial restrictions which are essential to continued production of saleable vehicles. A tank would be the ideal safety machine, but too dear and unsaleable.

Another continuing programme is concerned with the important aspect of pollution from vehicle exhausts, and a Mercedes V8 watercooled diesel truck engine of 12,760 c.c., the OM 402, using direct

1

2

injection, showed a carbon monoxide content in the exhaust only one-tenth of that allowed by the strict 1973 California test. Unburnt hydrocarbons and nitric oxides were less than half those permitted in the California test, yet the engine produced 256 DIN bhp at 2,500 rpm and weighed 780 kg.

Another disturbing aspect of the heavy vehicle is noise, and Mercedes have also produced a virtually silent bus, in which the loudest noise is made by the tyres. This model, the O 305 diesel bus, has the normally-exposed bottom half of the engine encased in a special cover, and the bus is only one-third as noisy as a standard vehicle. Experiments have also been made with vehicles driven by Liquid Petroleum Gas.

Another experiment to reduce pollution has been tried with a bus with hybrid drive, which can be driven by an electric motor from large batteries, giving no exhaust fumes in towns, or on the open road the diesel charging engine can be switched on while the electric drive

(1) Three splendid examples of Mercedes sporting machines that add comfort to performance. The models from left to right are: 280SL, 380SL and a 500SL featuring a rear spoiler.
(2) Shown here is the 1955 300SL belonging to former world champion John Surtees. The inclined engine made a low bonnet line possible on these cars, thus giving them a sleek appearance.
(3) The 300SL in open roadster form is the rarer of the two types. Note the

redesigned headlamp cluster on this 1955 model, a form that was to be used on later cars. This example is the property of Peter Agg. (4) The modern Mercedes interpretation of the sporting theme embodied in the 350SL (sports light). A 3.5 litre V8 power unit is used in this areodynamically styled car, in which the hard-top can be removed for convertible summer motoring. (5) The latest S series cars are possibly the most elegant design to date, shown here in coupé form.

3

4

5

continues. The company also have an electrically-driven bus on which a clutch of new batteries can be pushed in one side and the old ones out of the other, so that recharging takes no longer than filling with fuel on a normal car. Overnight it can be charged up from the mains.

A more recent development has been in anti-lock braking with which Mercedes experimented for many years before offering it on their production cars. This system allows the driver to brake hard in any conditions, but controlling sensors prevent any individual wheel from locking up, so that even a novice can stop as quickly as a skilled rally driver using so-called cadence braking, in which he alternately presses and releases the brake pedal to prevent wheel-locking.

This system is now expensive as it is in limited production, but is one of the biggest safety moves for many years and will obviously become cheaper and universal as more makers realise its virtues and fit it to their cars. Mercedes have taken a long time to perfect the system and make sure it is completely safe before offering it to the public.

7. THE SAFETY FACTOR

Daimler-Benz have eight major factories in Germany and seven abroad, the domestic plants making the cars and other products and the foreign ones concerned mostly with buses and engines. Most of the German factories are located in the south, where both Daimler and Benz originated, but the Berlin plant follows the same organisational principles and is part of the Mercedes community.

The emphasis on safety referred to in the last chapter is expressed in a six-point programme, divided between 'active safety' and 'passive safety'. The first heading covers positive features of the vehicle which help the driver to avoid accidents, e.g. good roadholding, easy operation, excellent heating and ventilation, comfortable seating, all to reduce the physiological strain on the driver, and keep him fresh and alert.

Passive safety relates to design features which can prevent injury if an accident should occur, both to those outside the vehicle and those inside.

1

2

3

4

(1) This view of the cockpit of the 350SL shows the high standard of finish to be found in the modern Mercedes sports car, where comfort is considered as important as performance. The 3.5 litre engine delivers 195 horsepower at 5500 rpm. (2) The 300SEL was introduced in 1969, the greater legroom of the longer body adding to the feeling of luxury. The car used a V8 3.5 litre fuel

injected engine. (3) Mercedes coupés have always been eye-catchers and this 250C is no exception. The two door design and resultant window shape make for sleek sophistication. (4) A 1978 example of the sporting 350SLC. (5) A 250 saloon coming to grips with the snow. (6) The powerful 185 horsepower twin-cam 280CE. (7) Reminiscent of the Grosser Mercedes of pre-war years, the picture shows the luxurious 600 with hood to the rear passenger section. (8) The much acclaimed 450SEL.

6

THE SAFETY FACTOR

1

2

(1) In pursuit of efficiency, Mercedes put this scale model of a car-caravan combination through a wind-tunnel test. The line created by the smoke is a pointer to the aerodynamic qualities of the car.

(2) Dr. Hans Niebold at the controls of the experimental C111-1V car which was used to test aerodynamic limits at high speeds. The car is capable of speeds in excess of 400 km/h from its turbocharged

The six point code covers:

1. Driving safety: Smooth straight-line stability. Good cornering through neutral handling characteristics. Perfect swerving control. Resistance to side-winds.

2. Physiological safety: Anatomically correct seats. Vibration and noise damping. Good heating and ventilation. Easily readable instruments.

3. Internal safety: Rigid 'safety cell' passenger compartment. Collapsible steering column. All parts upholstered or designed to deform on impact.

4. Visual safety: To be seen by other road-users in good time. Light bodywork colours. Good lighting front and rear. Good all-round visibility of vehicle outlines and traffic.

5. Operating safety: Strain on driver reduced because operation is simple. Switches are within easy reach. Controls are logically and clearly arranged so that it is difficult to make a mistake.

6. External safety: Front and rear body sections progressively deform- 3

able (crumple zones). Bodywork has no rigid protruding parts. Impact deflecting bumpers. More than 100 design features with a safety bias are included in each car.

Daimler's old garden shed workshop at his home at No 13 Taubenheim Strasse, Canstatt, next to the Kursaal, has been preserved as a museum and attracts crowds of visitors. The adjoining Canstatt plant built later, was destroyed by fire in 1903, and this was the historic occasion when the Mercedes Ninety cars for the Gordon-Bennett race in Ireland were destroyed, the company replacing them at the last minute by Sixties borrowed from private owners, which proved victorious, the red-bearded Jenatzy ('the Red Devil') winning at 89.92 km/h over 492.7 kms.

The Gordon-Bennett races were staged each year in the country of the previous year's winner, but Britain had a problem as no racing was permitted on public roads, so Ireland became the venue. France killed the series in 1906 by refusing to organise the event which they had won in 1905, on the grounds that France, as the principle automotive nation, should have five times as many entries as other lesser nations.

As already mentioned, the fire speeded up the move to Unterturkheim in 1904, when the first part of the new factory was opened. All passenger car production is now based there, and it also houses the famous test track on which visitors can be terrified by suddenly finding themselves banked at 90 degrees to the horizontal, looking at either the sky or the ground. The Sindelfingen works, nine miles away, was erected in 1915 to build aircraft, and later turned over to car body production. It was damaged by bombing in the second world war and rebuilt, in modern style, as the company's largest plant.

'Benz' old Mannheim plant was also turned over to aero engines, but today makes trucks and lorry engines in the biggest German factory for this purpose. The Gaggenau works near Baden-Baden, on the edge of the Black Forest, also had its origins in 1893, but now builds the cross-country Unimog vehicles and has a dramatic testing course, the 'Sauberg', made up of mud, wide ditches, potholes and stony gradients.

The Berlin Marienfelde works dates back even earlier to 1879, although the site has changed. Daimler electric cars, boats, trucks, and cars were once made there in the days of Gottlieb, but today it makes accessories and units for both cars and commercial vehicles.

Other factories at Bad Homburg, Dusseldorf and Worth also contribute to the total output of Mercedes. Bad Homburg now supplies parts like valves to Unterturkheim, Mannheim and Gaggenau, while Dusseldorf—once an Auto Union factory—now makes mini buses, transporters and steering parts for cars and buses. At Worth/Rhine, near Karlsruhe, the factory was built on undeveloped land, unlike the old traditional plants laid down by Benz and Daimler, and started production in 1964. It is now devoted to commercial vehicle production.

The suffixes added to Mercedes model numbers, like 180 for a 1.8 model, all have a meaning: D for diesel, S for Sport, SS for Super Sport, SL Light Sports, SSK is Super Sports Model Short, and the most famous: SSKL was Super Sports Short Light. SLR denotes Super Lightweight Racing Sports Car, as in the case of the 300 SLR which was so successful in the Mille Miglia.

In later years E stood for Einspritz or fuel injection and C for coupé, so a 280CE for instance was a fuel-injected 280 Coupé.

V8 petrol engine. (3) A 350SL is frozen to −25°C to test the cold-start capabilities of the car under extreme conditions. (4) Wind-tunnel tests are carried out on prototype models to determine the most efficient shape for future cars. (5) Stylists work on scale models of possible new designs, as well as a full-sized version in the background. (6) An aerial view of the modern factory at Gaggenau where tractors and transmission parts for heavy trucks are built.

8. RACING ON PUBLIC ROADS

The Daimler-Benz company has made sporting and racing models alongside its luxury saloons right from the early beginnings, with racers like the Pheonix and the first Mercedes in 1901, although of course these were from the Daimler company before the merger with Benz, who had his 1900 two-cylinder racer, then the Parsifal of 1903, the 1908 Grand Prix car, and the record breaker, the Blitzen Benz.

The very early cars were not racers in the true sense of the term, but production cars which were pitted against each other, and survival was the real test rather than speed. Differentiation between the touring car

(1) The slight wedge shape of the modern 380SEL is the result of exhaustive wind-tunnel tests. (2, 3) Old-style 6.3 litre 300SEL dating from 1968. Overleaf: A view of the Daimler-Benz motor museum which houses a fascinating collection of the firm's cars. Inset top left shows a fine example of the 500K supercharged special roadster. Inset bottom left: a beautifully preserved SSK which is in private hands. Inset top right: A pristine 1934-36 type 500K special roadster. Bottom right: a 1936-39 supercharged Mercedes 540K. The museum has examples of cars that date back to the beginnings of motoring. These include a replica of the first Daimler wooden-framed motorcycle, and the first cars from 1885-86, together with many other splendid specimens.

1

and the sports or racing car came later, although no-one has produced a better definition of a sports car than the man who said it was one he could not walk through wearing his top hat.

Daimler's early Mercedes cars did have a sporting image, as can be deduced from the fact that the very first one was produced to compete in the Nice speed week, where it was victorious. Not too much is said about its lack of success slightly earlier in the Pau races, but one does not expect a prototype to win straight away.

The Mercedes Sixty and Ninety both made a great impression in their day, but the Blitzen Benz, sometimes called the 200 horsepower, was the first pure record car which, driven by Bob Burman, set a world record at Daytona, Florida, of 228.1 km/h, the fastest speed by a road vehicle over one mile. This stood until 1924. The Blitzen Benz was a brutal beast with a giant 21.5 litre engine of only four cylinders producing 200 horsepower at only 1,500 rpm with a top speed, as

recorded, of 228 km/h. It was driven by side chains to the rear wheels in the manner of the day.

There were many Mercedes record-breakers after this, but they were mostly faired-in versions of racing or sports cars, apart from the enclosed-cabin vehicle in which Caracciola achieved 317.5 km/h at Gyon in Hungary in 1934, and the 5.6 litre record car of 1938 which was completely enclosed, wheels included, like a land speed record car. This one did the flying mile at 399.6 km/h, again with Caracciola at the wheel.

The very early races were on public roads between towns, like the Paris-Madrid (which ended at Bordeaux because of accidents), Paris-Bordeaux, Berlin-Leipzig-Berlin and so on. The idea of racing on enclosed tracks came later, although the world's first such special course at Brooklands in England opened in 1907, and Indianapolis in the United States a few years later.

GC 96

RACING ON PUBLIC ROADS

These pages show a selection of the beautiful cars, particularly convertibles or drophead coupés, that Mercedes have produced over the years. (1) Picture shows the 280SE 3.5 litre convertible with its now somewhat dated lines. (2, 3) Made from 1956 to 1959, the 220S had a 2195 cc six-cylinder engine developing 100 horsepower at 4800 rpm. (4) The classic 300SL shown against the much later SL model featuring the four-headlamp arrangement. (5, 6, 7.) The 300S was faster than the invincible pre-war supercharged seven-litre models. It had an engine half the size of its predecessor but was one ton lighter and, except for the fuel-injected Sc model, it used three carburettors.

1

2

3

4

There was even a St. Petersburg-Moscow race won by Hemery in a 120 horsepower Benz which averaged 80.6 km/h in 1908. This was another chain-driven monster of 12 litres capable of 100 miles an hour, a frightening thought in such a crude machine, open to the elements with no weather protection and the fragile tyres of the time. It carried two spares strapped behind the bolster petrol tank on the back.

The Mercedes 1-2-3 in the French Grand Prix of 1914 has already been mentioned, but sport came to an end until Germany was permitted to return in 1921, and Sailer won the Coppa Florio at 57.9 km/h in a Mercedes 28/95, a six-cylinder shaft-drive machine of 7.27 litres offering 95 hp at 1,800 rpms for a maximum speed of 110 km/h. This car incorporated wings and was described as a sports car rather than a racer.

In the early 'twenties Mercedes came back to racing with 1.5 and two-litre cars and others based on the 1914 winners and won two places at Indianapolis in 1923. The following year they entered the Italian Grand Prix but failed to start after Count Zborowski had a fatal accident in practice. Benz meanwhile were also active and in 1923 had the Tropfenwagen, a pear-drop shaped rear-engined car with six cylinders and overhead camshafts and swing-axle independent rear suspension, producing 90 bhp from two litres at 5,000 rpm and 100 miles an hour. The ran fourth and fifth at Monza.

We have already seen the success of the Silver Arrow racers, the W25's so-called because their paint had to be scraped off to get them inside the 750 kg weight limit of the formula, and the later W125 and W154, but the cars which live in the popular imagination are the sports

(1) A rear end view of 280SE, 380SE and 500SE models leaving the factory. (2) The elegant and fast SEL coupé with distinctive centre star. (3) A comparison of *aerodynamic qualities. (4) The 280S in Tatra mountain setting. (5) The record-breaking C111-111 diesel car in the wind-tunnel at Untertürkheim.*

models from 1927 onwards, beginning with the 26/120/180. The first figure was the taxable horsepower, the second developed horsepower without supercharger, and the third figure the power with the blower cut in.

On the road cars, the blower worked from the throttle pedal when fully depressed, and was not supposed to be used for more than 20 seconds, as overheating and consequent head gasket problems might arise.

Critics said the supercharger made a lot of noise to encourage the drivers to think they were going faster, and others referred to the adolescent scream of the blower, but it did confer performance for

overtaking at enormous cost in fuel. The ultimate development of the model was the SSKL, known in England as the 38/250, with which Caracciola achieved such brave results, although it was outmoded by the early 'thirties.

The 500 series, like the 500K roadster, and the later 540K, have a brutal appeal for their massive proportions, and were the ultimate development of the big, blown six-cylinder cars. The Grosser Mercedes of 1937 was one of the biggest cars ever made, and the name was revived for the postwar 600 which can seat four in the back facing each other to play cards.

The modern models are no doubt much better cars in every respect, but will never have the glamorous appeal of those giant convertibles with superchargers making loud screaming noises as two tons of automobile roared past ordinary mortals in slower machines. The chromium-plated outside exhausts may not have served much purpose but they did have eye-appeal.

1

2

3

9. A METEORIC COMEBACK

The Daimler-Benz company has defined its policy in the following terms: 'No-one building a world class automobile can let himself be influenced by modish trends. Our aim is the best possible technical achievement. Greater safety and more comfort, excellent driving characteristics and high-class workmanship, good engine performance and long service-life, easy handling and bodywork styling which will not be overtaken by fashion but remain unaffected by it.'

Development of Mercedes cars over the years since the 1926 merger of Daimler and Benz illustrates how closely the company has stuck to its aims. The original Stuttgart and Mannheim models, of course, bear no relation to what followed in appearance, but almost from the first swing-axle model, the 1931 T170, the family likeness began to emerge.

Certainly by 1937 one could see the shape of things to come in the six-cylinder 320 limousine of 3.21 litres which produced 55 bhp at 3,500 rpm for a top speed of 116 km/h, slow by today's standards, but

not in its day. The war years made a big gap in the model range, and the company in a 1945 statement said: 'Daimler Benz has ceased to exist.'

But they made a meteoric comeback in the course of the German miracle, and by 1949 the 170S limousine—an old name back again—had moved closer in shape to the Mercedes we know today. Although this was only a four-cylinder of 1.8 litres with 52 bhp at 4,000 rpm, it was faster than the earlier six, with a 120 km/h top speed.

From then on, the emergence of the Mercedes shape is obvious, from the rather heavy styling of the 1954 limousine 300, now a 100 mile-an-hour car with 125 bhp from three litres, on to the 220 series of 1954 onwards which founded the later line that has gone on in modified form through so many series. By 1958/59 the cars were becoming less bulbous and more squared-off in form, as the profile of the 180 and 190 shows.

From the time of the 1930 model 170 already mentioned, the policy was to extend the refinements already found on the larger cars, to what

(1) A rear-end view of the 170S cabriolet developed from the saloon. The 170 was made in 1935 and, again, in almost indistinguishable form in 1949-52. The standard post-war models were the saloon, convertible and convertible saloon or cabriolet. (2) A head-on view of the 170S, the designation given to the post-war model. (3) The threequarter profile view of the car shows running-boards, hood irons and front and rear retracting windows. (4) Passenger side view of this left-hand-drive car. (5) A close-up of the famous three-pointed star and star and laurel wreath symbol that dates back to the amalgamation of the Daimler and Benz companies in 1926. (6) Detail shot of spare-wheel cover. (7) Instrument panel and large diameter steering-wheel of the 170S. (8) The 170S was powered by a 1.7 litre four-cylinder side-valve engine.

4

6

7

8

A METEORIC COMEBACK

1

2

3

4

the company called the small Mercedes, and to provide more comfort, power and driving safety. The swing-axle independent rear suspension is criticised in modern times, but in its day was a giant step forward, which was retained until 1953 and later. The 170 pioneered overdrive, four-wheel hydraulic brakes, thermostat, and central chassis lubrication. There were diversions from the main theme, like the 150 sports car of 1934, which was not the best-looking car the company had made, and was rear-engined like the 170H which followed. But after this the line was established and the central backbone chassis, as on the 170H, disappeared in favour of the massive pressed box-section as in the 1933 380 model, until the chassis gave way to the pressed-steel bodyshell, which is universal today.

The diesel first appeared in 1934, first of a long line of Mercedes taxis which have served the railway stations of Europe for generations. In today's conditions of high-priced petrol, the diesel is booming in the private car sector; less in Britain than in most other countries because of the taxation policy, which does not give as much benefit to the diesel user as in some Continental countries.

Mercedes also produced a diesel aero-engine in the 'twenties, some

of which, in 16-cylinder form as the D B 602 of 88 litres, powered the famous Hindenburg airship and the Graf Zeppelin II, as well as speed boats of the German navy; a wide span of activity. Later versions around 1937 produced 2,500 bhp. The 12-cylinder water-cooled V engines powered the Heinkel He 100 V8 which took the world speed record, and this was improved upon by Captain Fritz Wendel in a Messerschmitt Me 209 VI to 755.1 km/h which stood for 30 years.

Aero engines were built at the Berlin-Marienfelde and Genshagen plants, the latter also near Berlin, with development work at Unterturkheim. Mercedes engines also powered the Heinkel and Junkers 52 bomber.

One of the problems in 1945 was lack of communications between different factories, which were in different occupation zones, but a new start was made, staff recalled, and the company came back to life, originally with vehicle repair work. By 1948 production was possible again, and the three-pointed star was on world markets once more.

The first cars were naturally re-vamped prewar models, like the 170S, but very soon there were some handsome versions like the 300 Sc two-seater roadster of 1956, now a sought-after classic. There was also a

A METEORIC COMEBACK

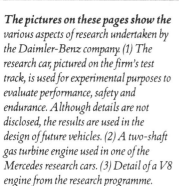

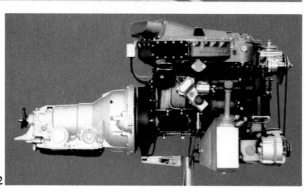

The pictures on these pages show the various aspects of research undertaken by the Daimler-Benz company. (1) The research car, pictured on the firm's test track, is used for experimental purposes to evaluate performance, safety and endurance. Although details are not disclosed, the results are used in the design of future vehicles. (2) A two-shaft gas turbine engine used in one of the Mercedes research cars. (3) Detail of a V8 engine from the research programme.

good-looking closed coupé, or fixed head as we call it, on the 220 of 1954. A comparison of power outputs shows that they advanced from the 2.4 horsepower per litre of the 1886 Daimler up to 175 horsepower in the 300Sc of 1955 with fuel injection, which put out 58.41 horsepower per litre.

In racing engines, the increase was from 3.49 hp per litre in the twin-cylinder Daimler of 1894 to 170.12 per litre in the 1.5 litre eight-cylinder supercharged racers which won in Tripoli in 1939. This was unbeaten by postwar cars.

Mercedes broke new ground with the Unimog four-wheel drive cross-country vehicle in 1948, and have followed up in 1981 with the introduction to the British market of the G-car or *Gelandewagen,* a cross-country rival to the Range Rover with the advantage that all changes of gear range can be made on the move, a facility which other cross-country cars do not provide. Mercedes describe it as 'a Fell runner in a Savile Row Suit', and it can be had in either petrol or diesel form. Just as the *gelandewagen* became the G-car, the *'Universales Motorgerat'* became the Unimog, and both serve the same purpose of offering

off-road transport for the farmer, allied to road ability.

10. A SMALLER MERCEDES

The modern S class Mercedes is as good a car as one can find anywhere, and better than most. The company has built up a reputation for expensive luxury cars of very high performance and of outstanding engineering merit. These continue to sell well, but the future lies undoubtedly in a lesser kind of car, less imposing that is, but still outstanding from an engineering point of view and offering much greater economy.

This trend will be imposed upon Mercedes by world conditions, as already in many countries owners do not like to be seen driving very luxurious and expensive cars, which lay them open to criticism by their workers, if they are in business, for a public display of opulence is not in keeping with the way most people think today.

But Mercedes will not be caught out of step with the trend, as they have always been in advance of most companies with their engineering developments; always probing into possible alternatives to what they

7

The motor can run on a reduced number of cylinders thus giving greater economy. (4) A new four-cylinder engine in which cross-flow principles are used by opposing the inlet and exhaust ports. Newly designed spark plugs allow for good gas flow through the large-diameter exhaust ports. (5-8) Auto 2,000 was the title given to a project sponsored by the German Ministry of Technology to seek information about the future of the car. The Daimler-Benz version was aimed at the long-distance touring car section, and was largely based on the S-class floor pan and mechanical components. From the front it bears a striking resemblance to the new SEC coupé models. Various engine possibilities are under consideration including a V6 diesel and a gas-turbine.

8

A SMALLER MERCEDES

1

2

3

4

(1) No doubt spurred on by the various estate car conversions to their vehicles, Mercedes introduced the T car, the first factory-made station wagon. (2) The 300TD estate is fitted with a turbocharged diesel engine as used in many lorries. Diesel engined cars have been produced by the company since long before the war, and Daimler-Benz are world-leaders in compression engine design. (3) The elegant T-wagons are availabe in five different engine versions. (4) A T model car being crashed into a wall during simulated accident research. Data from these experiments is used in the development of new safety features such as crumple zones and reinforced passenger cabins. (5-8) The new Gelandewagen, or G-car, marks Mercedes' entry into the growing cross-country vehicle market. Four different versions of the car are currently available.

have already. For instance, they have long been investigating the possible use of hydrogen as a fuel, in addition to research and practical experiments with gas and electricity as power sources.

The 'small Mercedes' has long been rumoured, but its final form will not be decided until all possibilities have been tried and the best format decided on. The company has some affinity with Rolls-Royce in the way it experiments for a long time before committing itself to a new piece of equipment. ABS or anti-lock braking is a case in point, as the system was under investigation for many years before being offered to the public.

Mercedes have long experience of diesel engines, and their 1968 range, for example, offered models with outputs from ten horsepower up to 4,500, and it may be that the turbocharged diesel engine will offer the power unit of the future in their smaller car, when it comes. Petrol injection was first used in the 1954 300SL, and this high-performance car led, with aid from the Robert Bosch company, to the tamer version applied to the 220 series of road cars.

The company's range has always been wide, as in the 1963 example of cars as different as the 230SL sports car which was small and compact, and the Grosser Mercedes 600 with room for four in the back and four windows each side. The company were almost unique in offering a four-speed automatic transmission when all the others (curiously again except Rolls-Royce) had three, but later Mercedes conformed, as the variable ratio of the torque converter makes three ratios adequate with a reasonable-sized engine.

There is virtually no field in which the company have not been leaders, whether in engines, transmissions, brakes, steering or the more mundane bodywork. When what they called the 'new generation' car was offered to the public in 1968, there were five years of development behind it, which illustrates the degree of forward planning required if the new model is not to be obsolete before it is on the market. In spite of the performance image, the cars were not designed for the highest maximum speed, but to offer good engine torque, to keep moving in the traffic stream smoothly and with flexibility.

5

6

7

8

A SMALLER MERCEDES

(1) The four-cylinder 2.3 litre fuel-injected 230E.
Mercedes pioneered the use of fuel injection in cars in the early fifties. The system ensures that exact amounts of fuel are introduced into the combustion chambers. (2) An attractive publicity shot of a 4.5 litre V8 450SEL model. (3) The 200D is a popular diesel model. The advantages of the compression system are: long life, cleaner exhaust, reliability and lower cost of the fuel. (4) The drophead 500SL sportscar uses the new 5 litre alloy V8 engine.

1

2

3

4

Mercedes have always taken the view that a car's speed must be related to its braking potential, hence the emphasis on the ABS anti-locking system ultimately developed. The 6.3 litre V8 engine used from 1971 onwards, offered performance not matched by many saloon cars. In the SL, the small sports car range, power went up from the four-cylinder 190SL of 1955, to 250 horsepower in the 6.3 litre V8 13 years later.

In the later 280 models, use of a twin overhead camshaft engine offered power outputs of 185 from the fuel-injected 2.8 litre straight six. The diesel, despite its advantages of simplicity, clean exhaust and economy, does not produce the power of a petrol engine. The three-litre diesel for instance, with a 21:1 compression ratio, was offering

(5) The fast 280S has a 2.7 litre six-cylinder engine producing 160 bhp. Strangely, Mercedes persist with the recirculating ball type steering, when most other manufacturers have turned to rack and pinion. (6) It is easy to forget the muscle-power under the bonnet when confronted by the sleek good looks of the 500SLC. The spoiler on these cars is not simply decoration, it is the result of extended wind-tunnel testing, and is intended to increase rear-end stability at speed. (7) The drophead 350SL, older brother to the 500, has a 3.5 litre V8 unit that produces 195 bhp.

5

6

7

80 horsepower, against 185 bhp from the slightly smaller 2.8 petrol engine, but Mercedes may have ideas about that for the future.

In 1946, when the company came back, they made 214 cars, and in 1975 this was up to 350,000, although they have never been mass-producers in the sense that some other companies are, and have kept the emphasis on quality rather than quantity. In 1976 another new bodyshell brought the smaller series, the 200 to 280 models, in line, in appearance, with the bigger cars. They were introduced at the Geneva motor show.

The biggest Mercedes engine in modern times has been the 6.9 litre V8 in the 450SEL, offering 286 hp and 140 miles an hour with zero to 60 mph in 7.4 seconds, which would see off many sports cars. This in a car

A SMALLER MERCEDES

(1) Before the arrival of the 190, the 200 model was the most basic saloon in the Mercedes range, if indeed such a word can be applied to any of the Mercedes machines. The car accounted for much of the company's production during the 1980s, its four-cylinder engine being a highly regarded power unit.
(2) The S-class cars are distinguished by their clean lines and aerodynamic wedge shape, as demonstrated by the magnificent SEC model. Windscreen wipers retract behind the lip of the bonnet to improve air flow still further.
(3) The 280S featured a revised six-cylinder twin-cam engine. (4) The

2

1

450SE is powered by an eight-cylinder engine producing 206bhp. (5) A new eight-cylinder alloy engine was used in the 380SEC model (illustrated) as well as in the more powerful 500.
(6,7) In keeping with more recent Mercedes tradition, the bonnet-top badge is conspicuous by its absence from the coupé and sports models. This is supplanted by the revised radiator insignia.

3

4

5

weighing 4,257 lb. Models for the USA have always been different in specification, and the 230/4 series of 1972 to 1975, for instance, had in its California version only 85 SAE horsepower against 95 SAE elsewhere.

In 1981 the Mercedes line-up ranged from the 200 series with five different engine options, to the 500 with five-litre V8 engine, plus the cross-country G-car, with the 230, 240, 280 and 300 in between; a bewildering number of types and models.

As 1982 came to a close Mercedes introduced the eagerly awaited 190 Series. The concept was simple – a small car that would fit into the Mercedes range and reach out to new customers who wanted Mercedes style and quality, but in a smaller package. It was to help in the transformation of the company, and only later was it to be perceived as one of the most significant model developments in Mercedes' history. The 190 was not the result of some sudden, stop-gap marketing

idea, but was well thought out and planned. High standards were set, and it was accepted right from the start that elements such as low noise, superb workmanship and good ride – qualities that had made the S type so successful – should be retained.

Though initially available with carburettors, and with fuel injection – the 190E – it was clear that this was just a stepping stone for a whole family of cars. The 190 used the 2-litre, four-cylinder engine originally launched in 1981, producing a lazy 88 bhp on carburettors and 121 bhp with a mechanical/electronic fuel injection system. Interestingly, the fuel injection system was so effective that fuel consumption figures proved not much different from the lower-powered version.

As if to underline the potential of the 190, Mercedes announced and demonstrated a very interesting newcomer, the 190E 2.3 16, with a

16-valve cylinder head. For reasons which will be explained later the car took longer to get into production, and enthusiasts who drooled over the promised specification and performance had to wait to have their anticipation realised.

At the same time the 190D, or diesel version, was introduced, with a new four-cylinder engine which gave the car a maximum speed of 100 mph, and by clever use of soundproofing proved a particularly quiet diesel.

Though Italy has always been the home of the innovative "improvement" market, Germany's AMG company, founded by Hans Werner Aufrecht, had set out in the early 1970s to provide tuning for Mercedes Benz cars. AMG were correctly to define a potential market in offering not only engine but body kits for most Mercedes models. Though only tolerated by Mercedes Benz, there was no doubt that the AMG kits became popular, developing a new sporting Mercedes subculture, and by employing them the purely functional styling on the various models could be sharpened up.

Left: introduced at the 1983 Frankfurt Motor Show, the high performance 190E 2.3-litre 16-valve featured an engine developed in conjunction with Cosworth engineers. A restrained rear spoiler hints at the car's lively performance.

Above: the clearly calibrated fuel, oil and temperature gauges, speedometer and tachometer on the Mercedes 190 E.

Right: the three-pointed star – universal symbol of quality. Although not standard on Mercedes cars, stop lights mounted in the rear screen are a useful safety feature, as on this 190E.

The "E" suffix on the tail of this 190 identifies this as an injection model, in this case using the Bosch LE Jetronic system.

Left: elegant alloy wheels are an option, albeit expensive, on all Mercedes models.

Facing page: boasting a top speed of over 145 mph, the 190E 16-valve sedan avoids the ostentatious approach adopted by some other marques. Modified skirts and a rear spoiler are this model's outwards concession to the sporty image.

Left: seen in profile, the 190 shows its clean, aerodynamic lines. The series had been launched in response to the perceived demand for a quality small car, and it soon established itself in the marketplace, comfortably holding its own against the likes of BMW and Audi.

Below: diesel units have been a stock in trade with Mercedes for many years, and the 2.5-litre turbocharged unit, as fitted to the 190D, offers diesel economy and respectable speed, but without the noise usually associated with compression-ignition engines.

Above: the high standard of finish associated with Mercedes was extended to the baby in the range. Apart from the engine, diesel versions boasted the same specification as the petrol-engined models, including the characteristically smooth automatic gearbox.

Right: simple, uncluttered instrument layout means information at a glance for the Mercedes driver, while the chunky steering wheel provides a safe and comfortable grip.

By the early 1980s AMG had built up a strong range of kits and products. At the top of the range was the long wheelbase 500 SEL, with the 5-litre engine tuned to give an additional 60 bhp, raising the output to nearly 300 bhp. To cope with this additional power they lowered the suspension and stiffened it with gas-filled dampers, offered a Getrag five-speed gearbox as an alternative to the standard four-speed unit, and increased the wheel and tyre size. So equipped, the buyer had not just a Mercedes but a car with performance and handling to match most sports cars. In addition to this were the body kit parts, such as front and rear spoilers and side panels, not only for this model but also for most other Mercedes. Warming to the new opportunities, they even offered a package for the Mercedes G-Wagen 4x4, correctly anticipating the expanding and discerning market for chunky, 4x4 cross-country vehicles.

AMG were not alone in this, for in 1982 the Belgian company Duchatelet produced the Carat, which was also based on the 500 SEL and was notable for its incredible paint finish, which utilised no fewer than 48 coats of opalescent paint. Lorinser and Styling-Garage in Germany also stepped into the field with aerodynamic and cosmetic body kits.

The ultimate alternative in the early '80s was the unique Mercedes 600, built by Buchmann for a member of the Saudi Royal family, and which was redolent of the 1930s, complete with running boards and old-fashioned style mudguards. It was some 21 feet long and weighed 2.6 tons, but clearly did not mark any new trend and, indeed, it probably remained unique.

In September 1983 the 230GE was introduced, using the mechanicals of the 230 series but with an estate car bodywork and four-wheel drive, and at the same time the 190 series was given a slight horsepower boost.

During 1984 Mercedes, like other manufacturers in the German industry, were hit by a six month strike, which not only dented sales but ironically led to a backlog of orders. It caused a slight pause in their development and launch programme, for their rivals Audi and BMW were creating an image which was attracting part of the traditional Mercedes custom. The introduction of the exciting 2.3-16, with its 16-valve engine, announced a year previously, came on the market much later than expected. The 16-valve engine had been designed in conjunction with Cosworth Engineering, so broadening that company's already strong international reputation.

Above: the 190D's "2.5 Turbo" badging suggests that the power unit lurking beneath the bonnet is capable of more than standard diesel performance. Turbocharging added 30 extra hp to the diesel unit, while superb engineering and excellent sound insulation also meant that the characteristic clatter was conspicuous by its absence from the D models.

Right: the downsizing of the Mercedes range, which culminated in the 190, was a direct result of America's stringent fuel economy legislation. New four-cylinder ohc engines, both petrol and diesel, were developed to power the series, while work on the body design helped achieve aerodynamic efficiency with a coefficient of 0.33.

Left: Mercedes' answer to the Range Rover came in 1981 in the shape of the Geländewagen. Shown here is the four-wheel-drive 300GD of 1986, which offers off-road motoring coupled with Daimler-Benz style and reliability.

Facing page top and centre: the majestic 420SEL, "L" for long wheelbase, is powered by one of Mercedes' legendary V8 engines. Boasting a wheelbase of just over 121 inches, the longest in the series, this luxurious vehicle is no slouch, offering a top speed of 135 mph. The 420SEL was one of eight S-class models launched at the 1985 Frankfurt Motor Show, quickly establishing itself as one of the world's finest sedans.

In the early 1980s Mercedes made the decision to develop the lower end of their product range by taking the 190 series in hand and developing it, so opening up a whole new market for a lower priced Mercedes model. At the same time, however, the series was expanded, and developed a character of its own, the 190E 2.3-16 being the ultimate manifestation of this.

Multi-link rear suspension had been introduced in the 190, but this was to spread to other models in the Mercedes range, and throughout the eighties the staid and somewhat hard external image of the Mercedes was steadily softened and refined, until it fitted in with the mood of the period without losing its classic identity.

A significant year for Mercedes was 1985, which saw the launch of the new 200 series and a new engine range for the upper end S class. To be fair, the engines were further evolutionary developments, as opposed to ground-up redesigns, but no one could complain of that as these engines were already fully established and highly regarded.

Appropriately, the engines were launched at the Frankfurt Motor Show that year, and covered both the familiar six-cylinder engines and the V-8s. For the latter there was an increase in capacity to 4.2- and 5.6-litres, and these engines were fitted in the now redesignated 420SE and SEL models and the 560 SEL. The six-cylinder engines powered the 260 SE and 300SE/SEL range.

Frankfurt also saw another interesting development in the unveiling of an estate-car version of the Mercedes 200 and 300 range. The estate car not only provided a welcome additional model with plenty of interior space, but also allowed the opportunity for Mercedes to offer it with their self-selecting, four-wheel-drive train.

The 200/300 range now offered six different engines. There was the four-cylinder 200D diesel engine which produced 72 bhp, the carburetted 1997cc engine producing 109 bhp – the workhorse of the range – and the 2.3-litre fuel injected engine. The 250D was supplied with the unique, five-cylinder diesel of 2.5-litres, producing 90 bhp, and then there were the six-cylinders: the 2.6-litre fuel injected engine offered in the five door estate car, with 188 bhp, and the three-litre, six-cylinder turbocharged diesel engine producing 143 bhp fitted in the 300D Turbo.

Mercedes-Benz looked forward to 1986 with considerable pleasure and anticipation. Not only had they recovered from the problems of 1985 and ended it with a high level of production, but 1986 also marked the 100th anniversary of the company founded by Gottlieb Daimler and Karl Benz. In those 100 years the company had, of course, changed, and in the twelve months leading up to 1986 Mercedes management sought to consolidate the company, both nationally and internationally, by investing in, and taking over control of, a number of companies in order to widen their portfolio and strengthen their position as Germany's leading industrial group.

They had a lot to be happy about on the car front, too, with the 190 range continuing to build on its already strong base. In 1986 this range was extended further with the 190 2.3E, using the four-cylinder engine in two valve per cylinder form with fuel injection. The 136 bhp produced proved to be ideal for the car, and most people who had experience of Mercedes 190 models were of the opinion that this was the best balanced model in the entire range, and it was no surprise, therefore, that it sold well.

In the same year Mercedes announced that they would build an additional factory at Rastatt, and this became a bone of contention in 1987, when the company was criticised for accepting one hundred million dollars of government aid. This coincided with a major shake-up in the boardroom, with the financial gurus taking over control from those more associated with product. It was a turbulent year for other parts of the German motor industry: the Volkswagen management was embarrassed by the apparent disappearance of money through what seemed dubious foreign exchange transactions.

If these boardroom moves at Mercedes appeared to herald a massive cutback in investment, events proved this not the case, for in 1988 Mercedes launched a huge investment programme of over two billion dollars, mainly in research and development and the modernisation of its car production plants. The 190's success indicated that careful research and planning was the key to future growth in the ever more competitive automobile field, and gave a pointer to some interesting developments at Mercedes in the years to come. Clearly the S Series of cars was due to be replaced, and work was already in progress for a projected launch in 1990. The new Rastatt factory was now in operation, producing some one hundred 190 models a day, which, since its introduction, had sold nearly one million units – surely the fastest selling Mercedes ever. At this time plans were announced for a proposed Mercedes assembly plant in Russia in the early 1990s.

Mercedes, who had been supplying Sauber with engines for their cars competing in the World Sports Car Championship since 1985, took over the project in December 1987, and contested the 1988 season as Mercedes cars. Meanwhile, in keeping with its more youthful image, the 190 was being raced in the German Touring Car Championship for production-based cars.

Mercedes slipped slightly in market share in 1989, and further substantial investment was announced. At the same time the company further opened up its markets by replacing its former cabriolet models with the exciting 300SL, reintroducing the designation of a model which created a sensation back in 1952, when it first appeared. The 1989 300SL offered a mouthwatering collection of new ideas, with automatic ride height control and damping, seat belts integral with the seats, and a unique electro-hydraulic operation to raise the soft top into position. To avoid the aesthetic shortcomings of a fixed roll-over bar, Mercedes came up with a concealed roll bar which would be activated in a remarkable three tenths of a second in the event of an accident. To complete the picture a 24-valve six-cylinder engine of 3-litres capacity was installed, giving the kind of torque that a sporting car of this type needs. As if this was not enough, the 5-litre V8 power unit was used in the 500SL version.

Perhaps the most interesting aspect of the 300SL was its coachwork, which was designed in house and was much softer at the front end, and round the wings and wheel arches, than previous hard-lined Mercedes models.

The 3-litre six-cylinder engine was chosen as the basis of the 300 E24 range, which was also launched in 1989. There were three models:

Left: crammed beneath the bonnet of the 420 SEL is the superb 4.2-litre (256 cu. in.) V8 engine. This lightweight fuel-injected unit delivers 201 bhp at 5200 rpm and a top speed of 135 mph, but all this comes at a cost of relatively high fuel consumption.

a saloon, a coupé and an estate car. The range also used a completely new five-speed automatic gearbox, the first of its type in the world. Clearly, the investment programme was beginning to pay off, and Mercedes were demonstrating that they were prepared to make a leap into the future.

The move by Mercedes Benz into motor racing under their own name, associated with Sauber, paid off handsomely. During the 1989 World Sports Car Championship the Mercedes team demonstrated speed, reliability and consistency throughout. A year earlier competitors such as Jaguar and Porsche were aware that the Mercedes push in motor racing had real purpose; the company came into the sport with the right equipment and drivers, clearly intending to stamp its authority. In 1989 that authority was well and truly stamped. What is interesting is that the Mercedes C9 car of that year still used a chassis that was based on the original C7 Sauber chassis of five years before, so underlining the originality of Leo Ress's original design. At the 1989 Le Mans 24 Hour race – thirty-four years after the horrific disaster involving Mercedes – the first and second places the cars took was honey on an already sweet cake. If Mercedes desired a copybook season to underline their technical authority, then they could not have asked for more.

With niche marketing the buzz word in the motor industry,

Mercedes responded by giving a reprise to the concept of the Mercedes 600 of the 1960s. The car they now produced was a six-door stretched version of the 250D or 260E models, so offering a business limousine for the upper end of the market.

During the 1990 model year Mercedes again moved forward by shoehorning the 5-litre V8 engine into a very much modified W124 chassis as used in the 300E, so producing the 500E. This car was clearly aimed at "out-BMW'ing" BMW, and its performance was formidable indeed, the car on test being quicker even than the 500SL sports car! It would be simplifying matters to say that Mercedes merely kept throwing bigger and bigger engines into the same chassis to create this car; the 500E was, in fact, re-engineered, with only the roof, bootlid and doors retained from the original 300E chassis. Even the engine was modified, employing a completely new electronic system using microprocessors, and different inlet manifolds, which combined to give the engine a mite more torque. The 500E is only available with the Mercedes four-speed automatic transmission.

Mercedes Benz therefore moved into the 1990s stronger than they had entered the 1980s. However, a general downturn in world economies in 1990, coupled with the Gulf War in early 1991 may well have shaken predictions, but should not affect Mercedes' long term objectives.

Above: leather and walnut bring to the interior of the 1990 500SL a standard of luxury rarely experienced in a sports car. No options are offered in the way of transmission, four-speed automatic being the only "choice."

Above: 322 eager horses reside beneath the bonnet of the 500SL in the form of this 5-litre, four valve per cylinder alloy V8 engine.

Above and left: radically different in body shape from its long-lived predecessor, the 500SL is a fusion of art and science, its distinctive wedge shape being both beautiful and aerodynamically efficient. Built on a wheelbase 2 inches longer than that of the earlier 560SL, the 500 is in fact some four inches shorter overall than its older brother, and weighs in at a substantial 4,163 pounds.

Above: a detail shot of the door shows the seat adjustment and position memory buttons on the 500SL.

Above: the 160mph indicated on the 500SL's speedometer equates to the car's top speed.

Right and below: the 500SL "roadster" shown sporting its aluminium hard top. When the top is removed, protection from the weather is afforded by a power-operated soft top. As a safety feature the car boasts a roll bar that springs into position when sensors detect the likelihood of the car turning over. The bar can also be raised by the driver, with either hard or soft top in position. Anti-lock brakes add to the car's many safety features.

Grace and pace distinguish Mercedes' magnificent dream car – the 500SL.